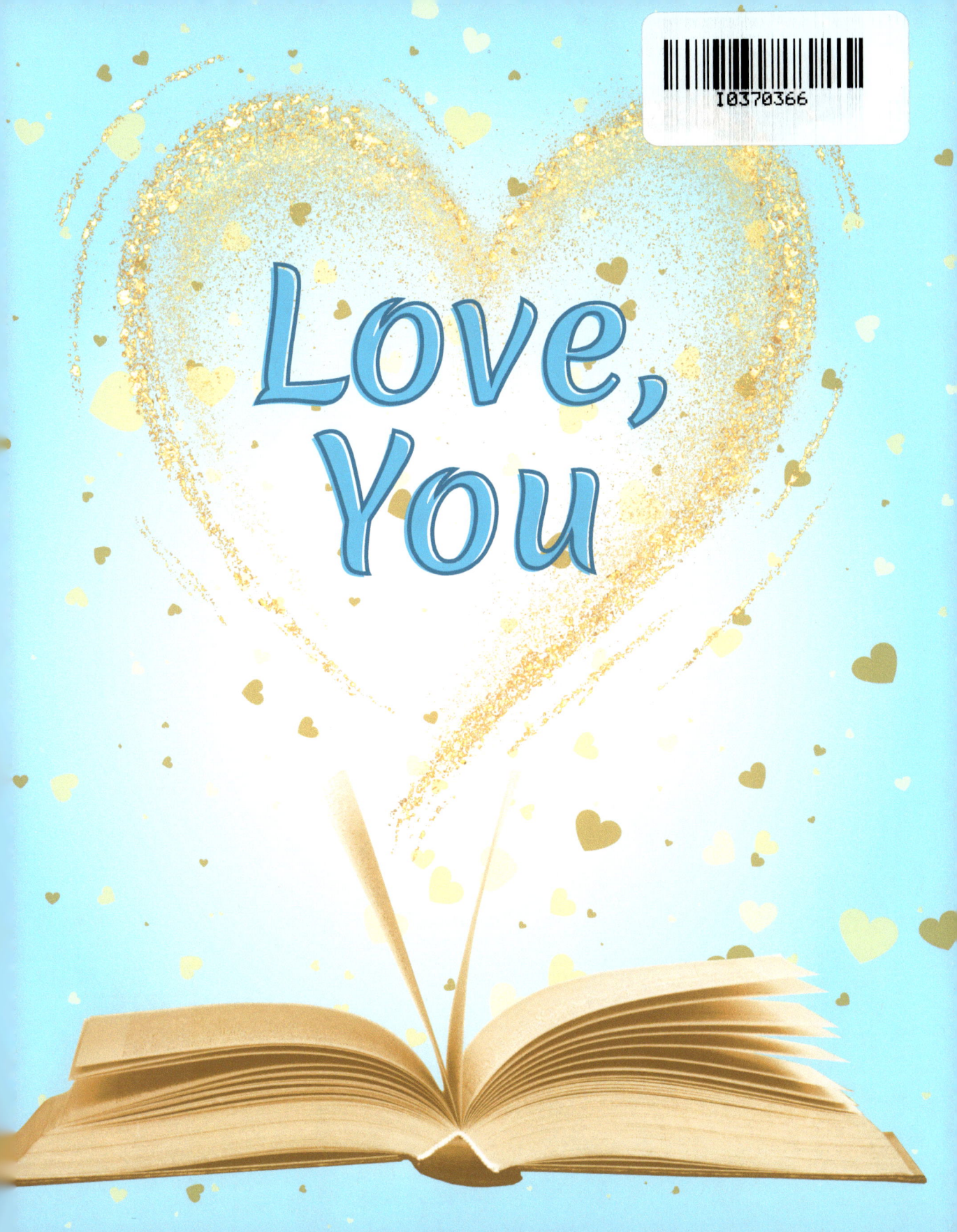

This book belongs to

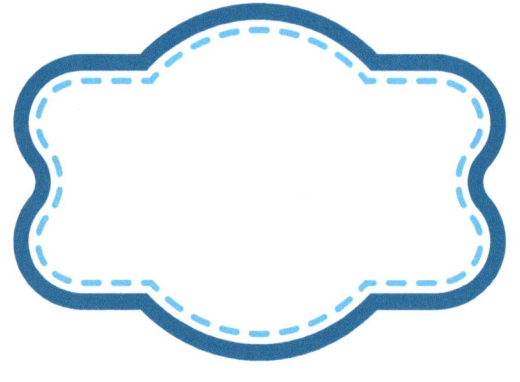

Love, You

A Youth's Guide to Finding Self-Love

Sarah Hanley

© 2023 Sarah Hanley

All rights reserved. No part of this publication may be reproduced, distributed, or transmitted in any form or by any means, including photocopying, recording, or other electronic or mechanical methods, without the prior written permission of the publisher, except in the case of brief quotations embodies in critical reviews.

Book formatting by Gareth Southwell
art.garethsouthwell.com

Published by Spiritual Flow Publishing

ISBN (hardback): 978-1-7750273-5-5
ISBN (paperback): 978-1-7750273-6-2
ISBN (ebook): 978-1-7380457-0-9

To Bryce and Blake,

I hope that you grow up to love yourselves just the way you are.

Love you,

Mom

Growing up is an adventure full of learning new things. You learn things like reading and writing, plus so many new subjects at school. You also get to find hobbies you like, and have fun with your friends.

But there's something truly important you need to learn too - and that's loving yourself! Yup, that's right.

You have to
LOVE, YOU!!!

As you get older, you can sometimes begin to compare yourself to others and feel like you're not as good, smart or popular as them. You can get down on yourself and feel sad and unworthy.

What if you could change those negative thoughts and start loving yourself for who you are?

It's like being your own best friend and cheering yourself on, because you're amazing just the way you are!

Some people might be thinking,
"Isn't that selfish to love yourself?"

The answer is NO,
it's not selfish at all!

Loving yourself means understanding how valuable and amazing you are. When you love and care for yourself, your heart becomes even bigger and more full of love to share with others.

Learning to love yourself is like having your own personal fan club, and the first step is treating yourself with love and respect.

Just like how you're nice to your friends, you have to be nice to yourself too! The more you love yourself, you'll feel like you can do anything!

Let's make a list of all the awesome things about you. You could write that you're a terrific artist or have a cute, crooked smile. Even if you're feeling down, you can turn it around by thinking of all the great things that make you unique!

ACCEPTANCE

Loving yourself also means accepting yourself for who you are, just like you accept your friends and family for who they are. That means accepting your magnificent strengths, and also that there are things you're still learning to do.

You can't always be good at everything and you don't need to be.

Also, if you make a mistake, don't worry, everyone does it! Just keep learning and growing, and remember that nobody's perfect.

Be Kind

Now that you know you're awesome, it's time to work on being your own best friend. You have to be kind to yourself and that means speaking nicely to yourself and avoid being mean.

For example, instead of saying
"I'm not good enough," you can say
"I am becoming the best version of myself"
Feels better, right?

Another example a lot of people use is, "I'm not good at this," but instead try, "I am getting better at this every time!"

When you use positive words instead of negative ones, it can change your mood instantly.

Our words are like a magic spell that make us more confident and help improve our self-esteem. So, let's practice using nice words and being kind to ourselves. We'll feel better and happier in no time!

magic

Let's make some magic words! Write down some words that make you feel happy and confident, like "Fun," "strong," or "kind."

-
-
-
-
-
-

-
-
-
-
-
-

Let's put the magic words into a special sentence you can say to yourself every day. This is called an affirmation, and it's like a secret message to yourself that makes you feel amazing!

So, if you wrote down the word "awesome," you could say "I am awesome!" Try it out with your own magic words and see how great it feels!

Make sure to say these statements out loud every day and really believe them. They can help you feel better about yourself and your life.

Loving you also means we have to practice self-care. Which means taking care of your body, mind, and feelings. That means doing things that make you feel happy and healthy!

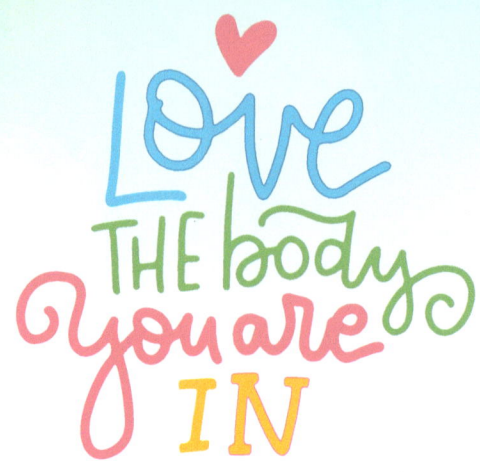

You can take care of your body by eating delicious and nutritious food, getting enough rest and sleep, and doing exercises like swimming or riding your bike.

It is important to remember that your body doesn't make you who you are. What really matters is how you feel inside. If you love yourself and are happy, then that's what makes you truly beautiful. When you feel good on the inside something truly magical happens! Your outside starts to show it too! It's like a mirror reflecting your happiness and confidence back to you.

To take care of your mind you can do things that make you feel relaxed and happy, like reading your favourite book, drawing a cool picture, or you can learn to meditate.

Another great way to relax the mind from all the noise and craziness of life is to take some quiet time and hang out with nature. Kick off your shoes, wiggle your toes in the grass or sand and find a cozy spot under a big tree. Relax and enjoy being still, as it will help you feel calm, happy, and recharged!

Feelings can be tough to handle, no matter how old you are. There are times we feel sad or upset, and that's okay. Everyone has emotions, and it's important to take care of them. You can talk to someone you trust, like a parent, friend (furry ones too), or teacher, about how you feel.

 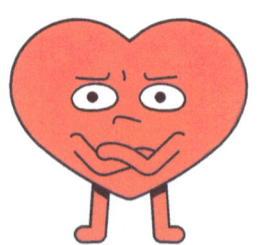 

If you don't feel like talking to someone, you can write down your feelings in a journal.

Writing can help you understand what you're thinking and feeling, and guide you towards feeling better.

When talking to others, it's important to remember to be true to yourself! Don't hold back or play small just to make someone else feel better. Express yourself fully and let your voice be heard. Your thoughts and feelings matter. There is only one you for a reason, so let the world see you for all the amazingness that you are!

Loving yourself means accepting and celebrating everything that makes you special and unique! When you love yourself, you don't need anyone else's approval to feel happy and confident. You know that you are enough just the way you are.

Self-love is a journey that lasts a lifetime. It's not like learning how to ride a bike and then you're done - it's something you keep working on and getting better at! Be patient with yourself as you learn and grow. Remember to accept yourself, be kind to yourself, and take care of yourself.

Most importantly,
never forget,
to Love,
you!

About the Author

Over the last year, Sarah embarked on a transformative journey of self-love, which lead to a desire to share the valuable lessons she was learning with her children. With her books, her ultimate goal is to provide children with the necessary tools and inspiration to become the best versions of themselves. Through her writing, Sarah aspires to guide young readers towards embracing their unique qualities, fostering self-love, and empowering them with the confidence to navigate life's challenges.

Books

 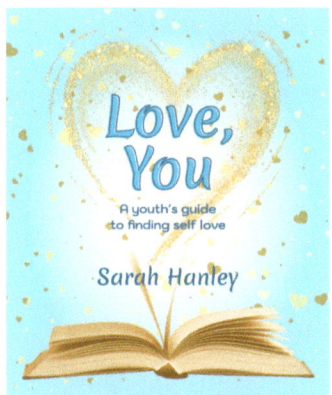 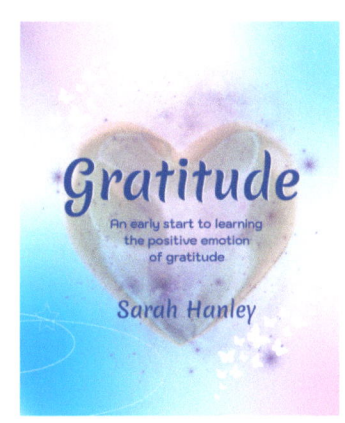

Journals

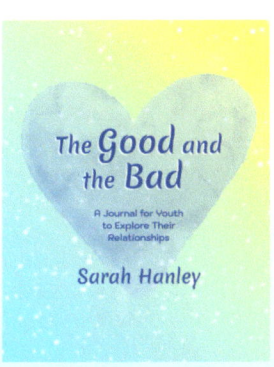 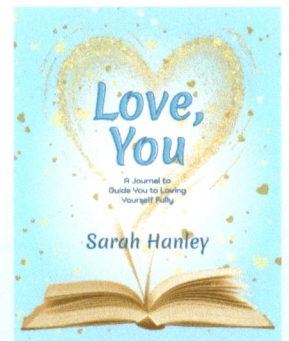 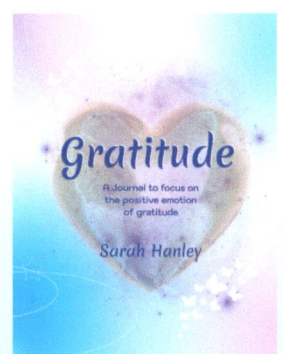

www.ingramcontent.com/pod-product-compliance
Lightning Source LLC
Chambersburg PA
CBHW042250100526
44587CB00002B/83